Shapeshift

Volume 52

Sun Tracks
An American Indian Literary Series

Series Editor
Ofelia Zepeda

Shapeshift

Sherwin Bitsui

The University of Arizona Press

Tucson

The University of Arizona Press
© 2003 Sherwin Bitsui

08   07   06   6   5   4   3   2

Library of Congress Cataloging-in-Publication Data
Bitsui, Sherwin, 1975–
Shapeshift / Sherwin Bitsui
p. cm. – (Sun tracks ; v. 52)
ISBN 0-8165-2342-8 (pbk. : alk. paper)
1. Navajo Indians—Poetry. I. Title. II. Series.
PS501. S85 vol. 52
[PS3602.185]
811'.6—dc21
2003005229

Publication of this book is made possible in part by the proceeds of a
permanent endowment created with the assistance of a Challenge Grant
from the National Endowment for the Humanities, a federal agency.

Contents

Acknowledgments

Grateful acknowledgment is made to the editors of the following publications in which some of these poems first appeared: *American Poet:* "The Northern Sun"; *The Iowa Review:* "Drought" and "Chrysalis"; *Red Ink Magazine:* "Nazbas"; *Spork:* "Apparition," "Asterisk," and "Atlas"; and The Institute of American Indian Arts Creative Writing Anthologies *Moss Moon:* "Gravitational Pull" and "Halo," and *Moonlight Draining Out of the Valley:* "Drought," "Chrysalis," "Noose in My Dream," and "The Hoof in My Soup."

Thanks also to the Witter Bynner Foundation for Poetry for providing a grant that enabled me to complete this book, and to Nizhoni Bridges Inc. for providing a residency during those initial months.

Finally, thanks to my parents, James and Earlene Bitsui, for their endearing support and nurturing; my family for their love, stories, and generosity; the Diné Nation for their continuing legacy; Sonja Kravanja for her uncompromising strength, knowledge, and insight in the development of this book; Phil Hall for his friendship and immense support; Arthur Sze and Jon Davis for guiding me toward poetry and leaving me there with it; Joy Harjo and Irvin Morris for their work, words, and comments; Valaurie Yazzie for her patience and love; and Melanie Cesspooch, Rulan Tangen, N. Bird Runningwater, Angel Lawson, Gabriel Lopez-Shaw, Matthew Shenoda, Frances Sjoberg, Jalon Begay, Evelina McGahey, Shin Yu Pai, Erica Lord, and the Institute of American Indian Arts community for their friendship, passion, and shared pathways in art and poetry. A special thanks to Ophelia Zepeda, Patti Hartmann, and the University of Arizona Press's Sun Tracks series for publishing this book.

Shapeshift

Asterisk

Fourteen ninety-something,
    something happened
and no one can pick it out of the lineup,
its rising action photographed
    when the sign said: *do not look*
        irises planted inside here.

But look—
    something lurking in the mineshaft—
      a message, ice in his cup,
        third leg uprooted but still walking.
It peers over his shoulder at the dirt road dug into the mesa's skirt,
    where saguaro blossoms bloom nightfall at the tip of its dark snout,
      and motor oil seeps through the broken white line of the teacher's loom.

Something,
can't loop this needle into it,
occurs and writes over their lips with thread;
    barnacles on their swings;
    fleas hyphened between their noses;
      eels asphyxiating in the fruit salad.

    Remember, every wrist of *theirs* acclimates to bruises.

Twigs from their family tree flank the glove's aura
    and asterisk water towers invisible,
while fragrant rocks in the snout remain

unnoticed in the bedroom,

because the bridegroom wanted in,

Pioneers wanted in,

and the ends of our feet yellowed to uranium at the edge of fear.

1868

Atlas

Tonight I draw a raven's wing inside a circle
    measured a half second
        before it expands into a hand.
    I wrap its worn grip over our feet
        as we thrash against pine needles inside the earthen pot.

He sings an elegy for handcuffs,
    whispers its moment of silence
at the crunch of rush-hour traffic,
and speaks the dialect of a forklift,
    lifting like cedar smoke over the mesas
        acred to the furthest block.

Two headlights flare from blue dusk
    —the eyes of ravens peer at
Coyote biting his tail in the forklift,
    shaped like another reservation—
        another cancelled check.

One finger pointed at him,
that one—dishwasher,
he dies like this
    with emergency lights blinking through the creases of his ribbon shirt.

A light buzzed loud and snapped above the kitchen sink.
I didn't notice the sting of the warning:
    Coyote scattering headlights instead of stars;

howling dogs silenced by the thought of the moon;
constellations rattling from the atmosphere of the quivering gourd.

How many Indians have stepped onto train tracks,
    hearing the hoofbeats of horses
    in the bend above the river
        rushing at them like a cluster of veins
scrawled into words on the unmade bed?

In the cave on the backside of a lie
    soldiers eye the birth of a new atlas,

one more mile, they say,
                one more mile.

Apparition

1.
I haven't _____
since smoke dried to salt in the lakebed,
    since crude oil dripped from his parting slogan,
        the milk's sky behind it,
           birds chirping from its wig.

Strange, how they burrowed into the side of this rock.
    Strange . . . to think,
           they "belonged"
and stepped through the flowering of a future apparent in the rearview mirror,
visible from its orbit
    around a cluster of knives in the galaxy closest to the argument.

Perhaps it was September
that did this to him,
    his hostility struck the match on handblown glass,
not him,
    he had nothing to do with their pulse,
when rocks swarmed over
    and blew as leaves along the knife's edge
into summer,
    without even a harvest between their lies
        they ignited a fire—

        it reached sunlight in a matter of seconds.

2.

It is quite possible
    it was the other guy
        clammed inside my fist
who torched the phone book
and watched blood seep from the light socket.

Two days into leaving,
    the river's outer frond flushes worms imagined in the fire
onto the embankment of rust,
    mud deep when imagination became an asterisk in the mind.

In this hue—
    earth swept to the center of the eye,
        pulses outward from the last acre
held to the match's blue flame.

Mention _____,
    and a thickening lump in the ozone layer
    will appear as a house with its lights turned off—
        radio waves tangled like antlers inside its oven,
because *somewhere*
    in the hallway nearest thirst,
        the water coursing through our clans
    begins to evaporate
        as it slides down our backseats—
its wilderness boiled out of our bodies.

The Skyline of a Missing Tooth

1.
The ice hook untwists inside the whirlwind like a tail.

A raven's rib ripped from the electric socket
    heats the palm,
its rusted core bound by the apple's shaven hide.

Like a concussion cushioned between fingertips—
    egg batter congeals in cracks of concrete.

    The fourth generation of bees flee the unlocked mouth.

The stoplight blinks
midway between wing, beak, and worm
    unwinding inside braided corn husk,
    pulsing near the foot of the interrogator
        as he slams the gate shut.

The interrogator,
    Every atom belonging to him, says:
You there—hook and worm,
you there—carved pebbles tucked under the glacier,
your apathy grows like gray hair in these untied shoes.

The tundra's anvil and spine
    are flung back into the quarried pockets of the pilgrim.

The "safe feeling" blossoms next to the caged wren.

Motor oil trickles from the harpooned log.

The Milky Way backbones the nervous system of the stream the deer sips.

This is where I broke the ice,

broke the sun's neck,
     and the city raised its sunflower above a pond of gathered lice.

The storm took care of it!
Reached down, hammered them flat.
Walls erected, stoned down, down,
and as we fled,
     we unbraided our hair from the fan belt of the exhumed engine.

     One twin kissed the other in the uncovered wagon.

2.
We watched them unravel from their neckties,
and took the shape of rain clouds blotting out the noon sun.

In their houses—
     The long night gloved the mist inside our gills.

And I stained the plaques clean,
memorized each brick flung from the window,
     while roosters crowed the grip loose.

Who made them leap from shelves unnamed?
Made them buckle down low,
pulled out by their tails
    from between each lie cupped inside another one?

A spear was driven into it—
    Underneath the pilgrim's skirt:
        the skyline of a missing tooth.

At Deer Springs

Turn signals blink through ice in the skin.
Snake dreams uncoil,
                    burrow into the spine of books.
Night spills from cracked eggs.
Thin hands vein oars in a canyon bed.
We follow deer tracks back to the insertion of her tongue.

The Eyes of the Executioner

The ants beaded into the sand before me
vibrate the executioner's skin
when the rain bends each twig in his garden
    and his wife folds down the cuffs of his sleeves saying:
    No his fist did not become eggs,
    his eyes are still blue.

The southern storm
    soaks our tongues so we cannot speak.
    I search for pores on the heads of red ants,
stir salt rivers into spiral engraved stones,
hide them in the pockets of the *hooghan*
whose light stream and sand walls
now only hear the lone pulse of dawn and dusk.

I return home
circling the trails of spiders
muzzled,
        they awoke smelling ash on their teeth.

I return
      realizing
the islandless sea inside the ear of man,
who stretched barbed wire over these gray hills.

    A tidal wave throws a shell on my lap.
I pull it close to my mouth,

begin speaking:
"The palomino ran in circles for weeks;
he eventually sank the sky;
he bit the sun in half . . ."

The Northern Sun

I find it necessary to breathe the morning air, to smell the potatoes frying, and watch the ceiling smoke into soft, white abalone dreadlocks, when I wake up abandoned, inscribed with *never open, look into, or stash in the backseat of your car.* I wear a mask made from the map of Asia.

Search for me in a ravine, on a cliff's edge reaching for the sun. Find me on the hood of a car racing through stars, on the velvet nose of a horse seeking its dead master waiting with saddle and bridle.

It is necessary to see the reflection of birds on the temporary ponds of melting snow. Grandfather, you named each mesa: sister, brother, friend, and I steered onto the pavement not knowing that inside our houses, the rain would clear and our fragrance would leap from our pores and into the canyons to be covered by crumbling black rocks.

Sometimes the mud on my boot breaks over fresh carpet, the payroll forgets our names, while the insects on our lips find our hidden names inscribed on their wings, and we roll through thorns to find the patterns of our loneliness scribbled on our bodies like images of dragons tattooed on rocks in a Route 66 mineral shop.

After this, you will reach to scratch your back and feel nothing but a black hole, spiraling like the agitator in an empty washing machine. You will bend backwards with your mouth pressed to the linoleum, whispering, *sister, I need a sister,* but you will not be able to reach her. You will be ten inches away, and never have you knelt low enough to hear the undercurrent of a breeze lost to twilight summers.

The cigarette ignites the bedsheets, and I write my last sentence. Lamp shades cover me; my eyelashes wriggle in my pants pockets. *Your vocabulary is like the breakfast menu of a science convention.* Bricks ripple underfoot, the moon reveals her daughter for the first time in 28 days, born with fists instead of hands.

A writer breaks every pen he can steal from the henhouse; disappointed, he returns to the hospital and informs the nurses that he should be pulled from the flames immediately. He sweats, points at his right foot, and says that he regrets flying back to earth obscenely underdressed to witness what he calls a malnourished theater eating its legs for dinner.

Is this what I deserve: a white anthropologist sitting beside me at a winter ceremony? *Listen. Your people speak like weeping Mongolians.* Perhaps it is because we have been staring at airplanes too long, I tell him, that our throats have turned into hollowed-out spider legs extending over the rough wings of a salivating moth, who rejected its cocoon as a child, saying how ugly it made him feel to be in a bed that resembled an anchor rusting in the shadow of a feeble cloud.

This time we feel the padlocks snap. Prison inmates untie their imaginations, which can sometimes be seen in the high desert of Arizona, lukewarm magma flowing through the sky at a 90-degree angle. The last time I saw the sun reflected red, I was pulling a screaming baby from her clutching, drunk mother on Highway 77 at noon. As the mother bounced off the pavement, I shut the baby's eyes and kicked the dead driver's foot from the gas pedal. The rear tires spun backwards.

The beer in my refrigerator still smells like bread in the morning. My mother's goose bumps continue to make me shiver when she tells me to scratch her back.

The IHS doctors gave her some lotion, but it doesn't help, so we scratch and scratch and scratch . . .

I just wanted a decent cup of coffee and a cheaper view of the Washington Monument, which loomed like a bright sun stream in a forest where the dark holds you like the wind holds you in a desert canyon. The cab driver asked if I was American Indian. I said, *No, I'm of the Bitter Water People.*

The glittering world, this place that we fly into where traffic lights play tag with our eyes when we lay back singeing our faces with the light of passing freight trains. What's there but rum and Coke? Bottle walls standing knee-deep in confusion and rat traps disguised as dreamcatchers?

Five years ago, my language hit me like saw-toothed birds reaching to pull my tongue from my mouth. I didn't know what to expect when my grandmother poured gasoline on the leaves and then fired it, saying, *This is the last time I'll ever harvest.* It was the way the sunset caught her cracked lips, the way her lips folded inward, which made me realize that there were still stories within her that needed to be told, stories of when we still wove daylight onto our bones and did not live like we do now, as night people.

Somewhere in here, our minds glow like fog lights, a Coke can bleeds sugar, and the eyes of a turtle ooze from a high school water fountain. Somewhere in Chinle, Arizona, a blender is surrounded and pelted with gravel and cement stones by children whose parents drift through cheap wine bottles like steam rising from the necks of hemorrhaging antelopes.

Frogs smell rainstorm against a shield of ocher clouds. Two A.M., the first flakes of ash surround a family of beetles dining in the cracks of the *hooghan's* fading walls, the flashlight of a policeman siphons dark waters from the spit can of an old medicine man singing the last four songs of his life. Inward, I can feel the gravel in my veins soften.

Red Light

What was asked for
won't step into view.
Coyote jumps
    onto asphalt running west,
dreams reoccur,
lightning strikes
    the same nerve ending twice.

She Was Not Invited

This here
woman who "smells like a dishrag,"
grandmother,
her pigment
    "a violation to the city ordinance,"
will be better off *somewhere else,*
away from the cooling fan,
away from the shriveled bodies of our mothers and fathers
bending over red cinders,
reaching to break in half
    the coat hanger shaped like an unborn child.

I push her into the hallway,
her feet sliding like dry bark over floor tiles;
    two ravens swinging low to steal the bread crumb from the mousetrap.

There are tears on the asphalt outside,
tears on the dog that licks them from my feet.
I push forward,
waiting for the nurse to tell me I'm in the wrong place,
that the spiderwebs are left-over decorations from last year's Halloween,
that I've mistaken this building for the IHS again,
that the scent of rain makes men do these things,
that it's okay
to leave your old ones outside when it grows cold,
that it's okay to leave your house in the middle of the night
to visit her shoes now.

Trickster

He was there—
before the rising action rose to meet this acre cornered by thirst,
before birds swallowed bathwater and exploded in midsentence,
before the nameless
    began sipping the blood of ravens from the sun's knotted atlas.

He was there,
sleeping with one eye clamped tighter than the other,

    he looked, when he shouldn't have.

He said, "You are worth the wait,"
in the waiting room of the resurrection of another Reservation
and continued to dig for water, her hands, a road map,
in a bucket of white shells outside the North gate.

He threw a blanket over the denouement slithering onto shore
    and saw Indians,
leaning into the *beginning,*
slip out of turtle shells,
      and slide down bottle necks,
aiming for the first pocket of air in the final paragraph.

He saw anthropologists hook a land bridge with their curved spines,
and raised the hunters a full minute above its tollbooth,
    saying, "Fire ahead, fire."

When they pointed,
he leapt into the blue dark
    on that side of the fence;
it was that simple:
    sap drying in the tear ducts of the cut worm,
    his ignition switched on—
        blue horses grazing northward in the pre-dawn.

Blankets of Bark

Point north, north where they walk
in long blankets of curled bark,
dividing a line in the sand,
smelling like cracked shell,
desert wind, river where they left you
calling wolves from the hills,
    a list of names
growling from within the whirlwind.

Woman from the north,
lost sister who clapped at rain clouds.
We were once there
holding lightning bolts
above the heads of sleeping snakes.

Woman, sister, the cave wants our skin back,
it wants to shake our legs free from salt
and untwist our hair into strands of yarn
pulled rootless from the pocket of a man
who barks when he is reminded of the setting sun.

At 5 A.M., crickets gather in the doorway,
each of them a handful of smoke,
crawling to the house of a weeping woman,
breaking rocks on the thigh of a man stretching,
ordering us to drop coins into her shadow,
saying, "There, that is where *we* were born."

Born with leaves under our coats,
two years of solitude,
the sky never sailed from us,
we rowed toward it,
only to find a shell,
             a house,
                  and a weeping woman.

The Sun Rises and I Think of Your Bruised Larynx

Sister,
blue like the larynx of rushing rainwater,
I think of you when I squeeze static from the river's bent elbow.

I am counting:
ten to zero, zero to nothing
underneath the dawn oak
whose roots resemble your hair
after you've danced counterclockwise
around steel-rimmed America
and returned home
with back spasms and a foaming mouth.

Do you still want to bury your shoes
in the blue mountains west of the Rio Grande,
where white birds shout sunlight
    and people don't ask you to repeat your last name?

I tie my feet to the thinning hair of our old ones;
their eyes burn, staring into the headlights of passing cars;
they saw footpaths bloom into black-boned factories,
rivers into pipelines,
and children delivered by IHS doctors
without tongues, without the fifth finger.

I think of your cupped hands tucked into the petals of a mud-caked sun.

The raven browned by the winter moon's breath
releases its wings,
    stretches its neck,
resembles for a second
the silhouette of a horse's head
carved from the nugget of coal
found in your grandmother's clenched fist.

Bodies Wanting Wood

When the fire turns
I lotion my arms
The woman weaves a storm design
Smells rain in the canyon floor

The wind in winter sleeps between our fingers
During prayer
It is released and blows into town
A swarm of locusts with wings on fire

Nazbas

It came whispering in broken English,
a stutter,
a twig tweezed from the small of the back.

He reached to pull the apple from her mouth.

Was it *asphyxiation?*

Should she have leaned away
and not let her hair slip through the cracks in the book?

Was it just theory?
    An inflexible aperture?
Nazbas and zero
    not to be part of *this* conversation;
two mirrors reflecting faces waking inside a snow drift?

The beginning is always the argument:
    arrangements, patterns,
        who gets this portion of lamb,
        who gets to speak English as a second language.

Dogs lap rainwater on television during conversations of drought.

This first cycle begins with an erosion of memory—

voices within voices pecking eyelids with velvet beaks,
one knee down,
    the other filling its veins with damp, white earth.

Turtle

I.

We are speaking inside the nervous system
without nerve endings to call our own.
Children born with teeth chewing into incubators,
not knowing walls,
or the beating heart of an owl
 hovering over the gates in her belly;
 atop the white shell,
dangling,
 cursed,
quiet,
waiting for these chains to be snapped in half
by the beaks of awakened turtles.

II.

We turn in their beds,
 eyes the color of faded maps,
when the story calls through the cut in the north ceiling.

Outside the door
we blow songs over its warm stomach,
but it doesn't soften or crumble into bread,
its palms don't bleed when hammered to the floor either.

It wants to leap into the night
without a torch or flashlight,
 but the fire removes its skin
and clamps back its eyelids.

A memory is wrung from the sheets of a hospital bed.

III.

While lying face down,

    footsteps climbed to the surface of the map;

the snake bit back the knife of the witness

who shook through the keyhole of a burning house

after dragging the moon's sister

    across the floor of her amphitheater.

It took him a year to forget.

ANWR

When we are out of gas,
a headache haloes the roof,
darkening the skin of everyone who has a full tank.

I was told that the nectar of shoelaces,
if squeezed hard enough,
turns to water and trickles from the caribou's snout.

A glacier nibbled from its center
spiders a story of the Southern Cross,
twin brothers
dancing in the back room lit with cigarettes
break through the drum's soft skin—
    There bone faces atlas
        a grieving century.

River

When we river,
blood fills cracks in bullet shells,
oars become fingers scratching windows into dawn,
and faces are stirred from mounds of mica.

I notice the back isn't as smooth anymore,
    the river crests at the moment of blinking;
its blood vessels stiffen and spear the drenched coat of flies
collecting outside the jaw.

Night slows here,
    the first breath held back,
clenched like a tight fist in the arroyo under shattered glass.
But we still want to shake the oxygen loose from flypaper,
hack its veins,
divert its course,
    and reveal its broken back,

the illusion of a broken back.

Conquistador

He laments the sea of congealed blood,
jumps from two owl feathers,
"Ten more years," he says,
and we will walk the shore's twisted neck,
    growing wings after drinking milk from the horn of the snared bull.

Scratching his chest—
he wept on the saddle
and smelled boiled rocks bubbling to the surface of the sea.
    It took a new trail around him to get to the actual message.

Some said: "Invite him in,
        the less similar the boot,
        the more attached he becomes."

He made love a house and shut the door,
    kept everyone's pockets full
and walked toward flies gathered in the hornet's nest.

    He didn't know the sound of a back spasm.

It wasn't just another false alarm,
    this tug out the door,
this last unsettled acre:
a stethoscope under which his fever heats the room;
    a continent of clouds reduced to the last penny.

The woman who left him in the mud
heard him step onto the embankment and bark.
The horizon loosened its coat of ash
as fishes sailed through the door
eyeing him coldly when he asked to be carried

                              back to shore.

The Gravitational Pull of a Fishbowl

They have to clock in at the right time,
    before the ship arrives
        with her cargo crates of goat horns
        shaped like long, flat tears.

They *must* descend into the near dark
before the sea haunts its fur-lined belly,
before we meet in the undertaker's blue city.

Our frost-pinched elbows
reach at the air—
    wings that cannot fly.

I look into the lens of a fishbowl,
where my days branch toward the gravity
    of footprints leading away into
    the thick green plaster of moss on stone.

Thinking:
    Spring,
    that moon with legs of silver water
    below
        black
ocean's hungry,
siphoned into the noses of soft-veined sharks,
death sharks, who sign their fathers' names in braille
    on their arched backs.

The clock snarls,
wraps its faded mattress around me—
    I bleed my left arm,
        carving deep gills at the entrance of light.

The Scent of Burning Hair

I circle my shadow
at 5 A.M. when crickets gather in the doorway
showing their teeth and striped tongues,
silver eyes,
singing about a wind-blown desert
sinking into the waist of a setting sun.

I have become a man crawling over his broken fingers,
searching for a ring to plant my lips on,
eating cinders while breaking eggs on brother's white skin.

I have either become a black dot growing legs,
running from the blank page,
    or the mud that is caked over the keyhole of a church hiding its bandaged eyes.

The bed quivers;
it wants to become a spider again
and sting silent the antelope that leap over children
whose mothers abandon their pots
and follow hoofprints into the city,
smudging themselves with the smoke of burning hair.

Look! There between the eyes of the horizon:
    two crows waiting for our bodies.

Imagine this at 5 A.M.,
when the river slides into a silent city

stuffed with decaying corn husks,

when everyone discovers razors in the womb of this land,

and the sun decides which bridges should be covered with skin and leaves

and which should remain as goat ribs submerged in sand smelling of diesel engines.

The Hoof in My Soup Glistens

This house burns clumps of cumulus against its back.
Blisters in the core of a dime rubbed on my neck,
like rubbing the hood of a '57 Chevy with a bar of soap.
Or turtle shells on powder-scented rocks in a tub of lemon juice.
Black pearls dipped in salt sink into my chest.
Teapot hisses.

A cheetah has been pulled from its skin.

Translation?

Fruits devoured by their own seeds
increase their temperature when the snare is lifted above the breast,
like the foot you dragged across the ear, when they only listened to sons,
and no one besides them knew
that our names stopped breathing in the last episode,
that the breathing knocked caterpillars from branches
       and made butterflies freeze on the forks of their tongues.

When you have ten names for snow,
what is the temperature of each vowel in *photosynthesis?*

This place, he said, weakens the roof the rain punched with seeds,
    and again they raise their cups to the night sky,
their fingers trace the nebula of the roadrunner's beak
    and pierce their cheeks with it,
because—*They* were listening,
       They had ears in the marrows of their fist,
         They heard the last horse snort under its nameless rider.

Halo

1.

The sound of rain
drops
against the drooping bones of
    arthritic HUD houses.

The weaving woman's child scrubs clear
    his knees
       splayed with the thin black paternal shadows
       of electric power lines.

Lines bowing like life-long servants
meshing their hair—
they uncover our crushed feet.

2.

The child picks at his halo
dissolving the dark into black pepper
eyeing
    the pull of the full moon
    on the water
    from whence our clans merged with flaked skin.

The halo's fluorescence
illuminates red mesas
and evens my palm with the coasting
    sky hawk and the rising blue.

The sun behind my thumb
keeps my blood from forming
    icebergs in their hearts
    when Sumner's rank fingers are locked inside
    the stone used to pin the rooster's cry
        to the wind-blown
        wall of sandstone eyes.

3.

My one child
    marks our twin names on the cells of fish.
    They are stories of snow clouds shriveling
        like the palms of our buried mothers
    and the ruffling of our fathers
    against the barbed necks
of lines drawn between pigment and pores.

We are only atoms trailing the carved skull wrapped inside a sunbeam.

Dawn.

The Noose in My Dream

I heard songs when the cactus wren sipped nectar from the tongue of a cricket.
It was early:
I remember the noose in my dream
and a sailboat anchored to a dying whale
imitating a sunset when there are no moist legs to comb silent
or beds burning in the sepia-colored lungs of the inferno.

I heard songs
and noticed in the uncovered wagon
the mouth of the woman
who licked the brow of the white fish
who dreamed of gills
and was given a broken-lipped husband who cut silt from her tongue
and abandoned the knife
  because it followed him like a stray dove.

  She gripped the steering wheel so tight that they buried her with it.

I drive home
imagining a man suckling milk from the cliffs of Canyon de Chelly
  and dream the awakening of knives inside grandmother's cabinet.

In the rearview mirror—
a storm hisses onto the horizon
a ceremony pales then yellows

a plane arrives with mute passengers
calling a nation to drink water from the river
     underneath the race barrier.

Umbilicus

1.

I don't think it's the sirens this time—
infections glide through the body unnamed
like carbon dioxide between the toes;
it knows the design underneath a glass hoof
but asks nothing in return for the name of its garden.

Dug from the side of its mouth:
>a trembling finger pointing downward past the cross
>into the reed plucked from the sky.

I trace the engine's outline in the pond.

2.

Cold glides up the back—
the forecast warns of horses thundering onto the plateau,
>though the eye only sees crushed houses.

3.

Weaving blankets from the fat of lambs
gnawing through gates clamped tight in the mind;
a body was pulled from the snow last night.
A body calving skin cells onto cinders over shards of flint.

4.

I told her not to go outside,
we are the ocean and the rocks that waves slap open,

and all of us
in these classrooms were speared by the shepherd's single gray tooth.

I told her that he was out there
watching the doorknob untwist inside her mother's belly,
waiting for the police sirens to erupt from her cracked eggs.

I told her I smelled gunpowder in the curio shop
in windows overlooking inmates gathering under circling ravens,
in the entrails of clouds swelling under the belt of the Orion nebula.

Offering

There—fire on the hillcrest
angling left
drawing open a storm with thirteen moons left in its coat.

Fins grip flint lodged between my fingers.

The snow won't cover these pages.

Ten whips finally crack the spine
teeth burst
bread is offered
a plow in the cornfield rusts.

Coyote bones curl over river rocks and crumble into salt.

A tree line slopes over bodies
casting shadows between the pages of closed books.

Bullet Wet Earth

Pushing back the whip
I tuck and roll,
darting again
    from the bullets that smell of wet earth,
monsoon earth
    rising like foam through the fences that wound.

Last night a thorn flowered the imagination of a thorn;
a moth buried its tongue between my fingernails,
and a calf was dragged the length of my body.

My shoulders hang like a rainstorm over a bed that has become desert
as I have become:
    a dehydrated shadow born with scratches in his throat.

It's easy to drift through this desert,
one hand on the wheel,
the other
    pinching dew drops into seeds that glide into vapor.

The doctor said it was a heart condition,
and it's been two years of listening to the wind and only wind
    that is making our bodies yearn to be suckled by black stones.

I cover these pages with my fist.
Imagine skin meeting the lens of a camera.
    Hear a voice coming from the roots in the basket, saying:

"Come closer,
  swallow a handful of air,
      pour water over your feet,
      you have become a ghost without hands."

Nahasdzáán

Mother thought:
First we will run, then we will walk.
She asked, "Do we ramble when we speak in tongues?"

Her lack of supervision made this happen.

The dusk, the dawn, everything in between: a mistake.
The morning,
    her toothache,
the shovel dulled in daylight—
    all digging fire from shallowing rivers.

Her plan:
    "one big mistake."

In this language
she wasn't asked to sing
because in this room
there was never a light switch,
never a search for the memory of onyx
collected against the rib

      the origin—
               iiná.

The Four Directions of a Lie

1.
The rain
    mid-morning
scratching seeds from the marrows of bullets.

A brass door handle warms the palm of the intruder.

The suggested retail price of entrance
    hasn't yet cracked under the weight of our gravitational pull.

A pull to the nucleus of a lie.

Each nail extracted from the ships is driven into their palms
until they are only hands laid flat on the earth's buckled vertebrae.

2.
Two birds spit oil: sunbeam, soot, sunbeam . . .

3.
The rain clouds
    thoughts of milk—
books clam shut under the patter of blind children
    who cut their flesh with the hands of steel clocks
        and slide like melting ice underneath the church door.

But the door
with its fist full of light

wanted only daughters
who would ripen during autumn,
who would become the mothers of a drowned city.

4.

The last whisper heard this morning was not the shuffle of feet
nor the momentary pause in the tightening of his jaw.

It was the sudden leap of a deer when water rippled outward under his chin.

Some say it is *irony,*
others
a bear twitching in the hunter's garden.

Drought

1.

More drought, says the old woman digging roots from the arroyo bottom as the
sun becomes a spiral trail marked on a sandstone cliff that is now
                    a memory to the Maya.

A gathering of birds decides paths and rearranges footsteps, forming the
scribble of branches
and electric wires emerging from a cloud of red dust.

Where am I when I follow the satellite east?
Does the sun know that a rock soaks in a bowl of rice somewhere on the other
side of my palm? Does the sky recognize its feet when it is covered with light bulbs
instead of the eggs of red ants?

A child climbs the blue ladder that has just appeared in his dream;
his mother then wraps a clock with a white sheet and listens to its slowing pulse.

Two moths shake their fist at a young boy who unplugged his father's reading lamp,
a newspaper then makes the sound of autumn,
        a silver horse snorts—
the dark windows remind him of his master's eyes,

            the shadows of crushed grapes.

2.

I place a jar of teeth in the sun
so we can watch leaves grow;

after all, isn't calcium the color of our books
when we think of a cat purring over a bowl of milk?

A pale-lipped thespian slows his breath, crosses his eyes,
and finds a melted coin in a bowl of rice.

Will the person in the car approaching at high speed
slow down long enough to see that the coin was made in 1979?

A dog in the approaching pick-up truck licks his paws,
    fleas bite into our umbrellas,
and we find lightning bolts held between lovers who share the same clan
in two paint strokes on unstretched canvas.

Cinder blocks throb under our feet when we swallow fishhooks.

A church empties, eels are discovered swimming underneath the floorboards.
    Train engines stutter to a stop.
A priest sleeps on a coat hanger
    and dreams of feathered feet wrapped in stirrups
    floating through the eye of a needle.

3.
The noose in my dream becomes a deer and shakes dust from its eyelids,
it wants to cry for rain,
but we are keeping the rain in Styrofoam boxes at the bus station.

The grandmother was out there shaking a stick at the coal miners.
    That night she cried black tears
    and wove her hair into the feathers of a visiting night owl.

Juniper roots surface in the dishwater.

When one dreams of a mouth covered in white chalk,
speaking only in English,
it is a voice that wants to be cut free from a country whose veins swim with axes
and scissors.

4.
Tonight
the beginning   ends.
I singe the nerves of a camera lens smooth
because it captures rain
        that does not enter from the east.

I dream of lizards and bulls and watch a silver moth penetrate the window screen.

How do we remove our thumbprints from fences,
        when axes are left to grow under the sun in a bucket of water?
When the corn roaster goes to town grinding his teeth,
        and his wife discovers a miniature railroad curling in and around her pelvis?
Will he then run his fingers down the length of his gun,
        imagining a cosmonaut brushing his teeth in zero gravity?

5.
Each day
        the city grows an inch taller,
the children in her draw stares from planes dipping into low altitude.
        Do the pilots see the buttons their teachers have sewn onto their ears?

Listen, the gravediggers unfold the earth's bandages
and remove vacuum cleaners filled with killed pottery and broken arrowheads.

A cyclone curls around my fist when I approach city limits.
A boat is released from land,
covered with snails licking rust and salt.

We anchor our cars to a bundle of prayer feathers.
A train slides underneath the parasol of a woman beading her skin cells to
curved asphalt,
    sensing that we have finally listened
and are now strolling our televisions out the front door,
past the recently divorced mailman
and into the supermarket,
    saying we want our teeth back;
our fingers smell of wet ash.

6.

I turn away.
I must not look at the sweat beads of the snorting horse
or I will dream of being a wingless bird
lapping at the reflection of clouds in a rain puddle
left in the summer sun,
    shaking my beak at the mercury rising in the thermometer.

A child swallows water and does not wake.
Mother then rubs a book over his moist back.

Read this,
understand their language,
or sleep in a bottle of broken nails for the rest of your life.

The night sinks from my eyes;
mud men wash the earth from their knees;
a gate key is lifted from the gatekeeper,
who then pulls the doormat
from the drought's gravitational pull.

We descend into our basements,
searching the dark for the wet noses of our mothers and fathers,
but we find pencils and postage stamps instead—
no paper, no address book.
So we begin sifting through the ash of burnt hooves in a field of rust,
    but find only broken glass,
        coat hangers,
            and the shoes of a dying priest.

I Don't Remember:

horses
running
from glass
over
broken glass
into broken glass

Chrysalis

It wasn't the leaves that descended upon you
or the horse that knelt on the river's edge,
pushing his nose through mist,
    a root that wanted to peel itself into a flower.

It was ash,
dry as the skeletons of drained soup cans
on the river front
where a man's coarse throat bleeds
because the language is a dying thing,
covered in blankets,
    beaten with forks and spoons.

These baskets have become graves,
    a shot glass of tears tucked between the legs of a veteran,
a wristwatch pulled tightly around his tongue
so that he may savor this hour
when death drags its tail across the necks of hunted children,
who are shivering again under the sun's sharp chin,
half awake in a boat on a shore of gray gulls,
pressing grapes into their eyes,
drinking the wine that leaks from their shadows.

Cities break into sand before the approaching shovel;
their windows glisten in the soft light of the Milky Way
as I remember it.
    How young I was to read the passages of the Bible,

my wings caked in earth,
mud forming in my footsteps,
water seeping from my lips when he came to drink.
He came to drink and would not stop.
He was a bee pollinating the milky surface of the moon reflected in the rearview
mirror.

The deer blinked and all was well again,
calm as the breeze blowing through prison gates.
I shave the edges of my mustache and imagine cutting the policeman's arm from
his flashlight.
But still it did not stop the lions from sniffing the snouts of dying bulls,
or the red squaw from selling her jewelry in aisles of restaurants serving leaves
and grass.

And no, there is no one here.
This casket: the seed of a blood clot.

Bread dipped in gunpowder is to be fed to the first graders in that moment
when their hair is cut
    and a ruler is snapped,
and their whispers metamorphose into a new chrysalis of thought.
A new wing emerging from the lips of these Indians,
who are no longer passing thoughts in the paragraphs of an oil-soaked dictionary
but hooves carved into talons,
hilltops from which light is transformed into the laughter of crickets.

I want to remain here
where he doesn't drink my lips
or remove the cocoons my eyes have become.

Rattles erupt on the north horizon.
The harvester unties her shoelaces.
I see the sun, eclipse it with my outstretched palm,
and dig away my reddening skin.

    "It wasn't like this before," I tell myself.
When I am thrown into a florescent room where the sink hunches
like an eagle claw,
it stops,
pulls the wind to a breathing space the size of a mouse's lung,
and I am drowning in the air around my feet again.

Antelope are gnawing into the walls of the city.
And *those* Indians are braiding yucca roots into the skin of their scalps again.

I want to fall beside them,
count their fingers:
    five hundred and five rows of spilled blood marking the trail home.
The trail will not be followed again,
because there in the ears of the Indians
are echoes of the hissing belt
and the laughter of thieves
measuring the length of the treaty
with the teeth of the jury that is seduced by the glimmers of gold.

It is ash, all of it!
Fruit flies buried in the skin of onions,
canyons seeking the river that has left them orphaned,
cars cruising their velvet wheels over teeth and beaks,
eyeless dogs barking in hailstorms,

and owls, two of them coming from the east,
carrying the night between them: a wet blanket designed by a woman who dreams of
     lightning,
saying that we have finally become mountains
rising above a valley of weeping dishrags that cling to the ground below,
raising fences and crosses and houses.

And no, this is not about sadness:
the gasp of a mute who buries his legs in the arroyo bottom
when the first drops of rain pepper his forehead,
who earlier that morning brought a leaf into the front yard,
saying that we may grow from this,
we may inch into the next world
and rummage for nectar in the thinning bones of shadowless thieves.

This plate before me is made from broken tusk; this fork, the fingers of a rat,
and we eat leather in caves behind the train tracks.
These caves where our hair breaks into ash when washed
are a place of birth;
the first cry echoing from the amphitheater
was a song sung in thinning air.

This is not about the rejection of our skin;
the mud dries as it is poured into our ears.
But the linguist still runs his hands up the length of our tongues,
perplexed that we even have a tongue   at all.

About the Author

Sherwin Bitsui, originally from White Cone, Arizona, on the Navajo Reservation, currently lives in Tucson, Arizona. He is Diné of the Bitter Water People, born for the Manygoats People. He holds an AFA from the Institute of American Indian Arts' Creative Writing Program and is the recipient of the 2000–2001 Individual Poet Grant from the Witter Bynner Foundation for Poetry, the 1999 Truman Capote Creative Writing Fellowship, and more recently, the 2002 University of Arizona's Academy of American Poets Student Poetry Award. He has published his poems in *American Poet, The Iowa Review, Frank* (Paris), *Red Ink,* and elsewhere. *Shapeshift* is his first book.